HOW TO BE AN

ORDINARY HERO

*The Magic Key
for Taking Charge of Change
and Reaching Your Heroic Potential.*

DWIGHT LONGENECKER

Available from www.ordinaryhero.net

This edition published in the United Kingdom in 2005 by Transform

ISBN 0 9547321 6 2

Printed and bound in Great Britain by
Transform, PO Box 2178, Caterham, CR3 6ZT

We must be willing to get rid of the life we've planned,
so as to have the life that is waiting for us.
— *Joseph Campbell*

We do not have to become heroes overnight. Just a step
at a time, meeting each thing that comes up, seeing it is
not as dreadful as it appeared, discovering we have the
strength to stare it down.
— *Eleanor Roosevelt*

Life is a daring adventure or nothing at all
—*Helen Keller*

Contents

How to Be an Ordinary Hero

By DWIGHT LONGENECKER

"Before this course," Janet said, "I went to the doctor and my height was five foot six inches. When I went back after the course I measured five foot eight inches." Janet's new-found ability to stand tall and look life in the eye shows the transformation that had taken place in her life. Janet had taken part in our Ordinary Hero programme for victims of violent crime, and was testifying to the power of the Ordinary Hero programme.

Eight years earlier Janet's twenty-five year old son had been murdered. For eight years Janet had been locked in a world of grief, rage, sorrow and despair. She saw no way out, but the Ordinary Hero programme helped her see new possibilities. It gave her a way to glimpse a more positive future and set out to make her vision a reality.

All Change!

Most of us aren't in Janet's desperate condition, but we're all trapped in a world we wish would change. We want more out of life. We want to be healthy and attractive. We want a happy family, a good love life and a stimulating and rewarding career. We want to make a difference in the world. We long to understand the meaning of life and create something beautiful and true with the precious time on earth that we've been given.

For such wonderful things to happen we need to change. Part of us is desperate for that change, but another part of us knows that change is risky. As a result we hold back and play safe.

It's human nature to avoid the unknown. This is why we avoid change. We imagine that we can stay as we are or, if we're going through change at the moment, we tell ourselves that as soon as the transition is over

There is nothing permanent except change.
– Heraclitus (540 BC)

we'll be able to settle down and not have to change again. But this is an illusion. Change is always happening. In fact, in this life, there is nothing permanent except change.

Since real change is happening all the time the question is not, 'will my life change, but will I be in charge of the change?' The trick is to see that change is not a threat, but a great and exciting adventure. Once you accept that change is not only inevitable, but positive, you can take charge of change every day, and begin to make your dreams a reality. This book shows you how to get started. It really does empower you to change your world!

The Magic Key

The heart of this book is a simple story called *The Magic Key*. The story gives you a simple way for you to take charge of change. *The Magic Key* is a fairy tale for grown ups. Like every folk tale, it's full of magic, danger, adventure and romance. That's because change itself is full of magic, danger, adventure and romance.

Maybe when you read the words 'fairy tale' you said to yourself, "Fairy tales! I don't have time for fairy tales! I want facts. I want bullet points. I want step by step instructions for action and success. " Hold on! Don't worry. You'll get step by step directions; it's just that they're going to be delivered in a new way. You're not stupid. Once you've grasped the basics locked in the story of *The Magic Key* you'll see new ways of applying them every day.

> *The shortest distance between a human being and truth is a story*
> – Anthony de Mello

When you heard the words 'fairy tale' were you tempted to toss the book away because you thought it was childish or shallow? Stop for a moment and give it a chance. Many people have felt that way, but they've pushed on a bit only to find that they've got hooked. They found fascinating levels of depth and insight in the story. They started to see themselves and their world in a new way.

Once they got into the story (or the story got into them), they discovered that it had an almost magical power to help them change. How does the story work its magic? The way stories have always worked their magic. You'll go on an adventure with the hero, and as he discovers a new way of seeing life you will too.

> *The way we see the problem is the problem.*
> – Stephen Covey

How to Be an Ordinary Hero

Steve is one of the prisoners who took part in our *Ordinary Hero* © prison resettlement programme. Steve had been in and out of jail for fifteen of his thirty-one years. He came on the *Ordinary Hero* © course because he was fed up with the patterns of his life. He wanted to change direction for good.

Steve was given a copy of *How to Be an Ordinary Hero* as part of the Ordinary Hero programme. The story of *The Magic Key* gave him a new way of seeing his world. The Ordinary Hero programme helped him apply the principles of *The Magic Key* so he could see where he was, where he wanted to go, and how to get there.

Learning the pattern of change was only the first step. Steve decided to take action. When he was released he started his own car cleaning business. Taking that step wasn't easy, in fact, Steve said it was the hardest thing he'd ever done.

> *We cannot think ourselves into a new way of living. We must live ourselves into a new way of thinking.*
> – *Richard Rohr*

Steve resisted change for many reasons, but most importantly, he held back because he didn't know that there is an easy to understand map for the change process.

The Hero's Map

The map for change follows the outline of the world's great stories. Every story—from ancient Bible stories to the latest Hollywood blockbuster—follows the pattern of the hero's quest. The hero's quest is always about an ordinary person who leaves his or her comfort zone and enters a world of adventure to achieve some great prize.

The story of the hero's quest goes deep. It's written in the depth of every human heart and mind because it charts the way anyone anywhere makes real change happen. The step by step outline of the hero's quest gives us a map for change. My version of the plan is called *The Hero's Map of Achievement*.

The gifts we can receive from people who have tasted possibilities are maps which we then use to guide on our journey.
    – *Ram Das*

As you read the story of *The Magic Key* you'll experience this step by step outline of the change process. Each chapter of the story unlocks another stage of *The Hero's Map of Achievement*. For each stage there's a specially designed icon that illustrates that step of the journey. At the end of the book you'll find a picture that reminds you of all ten steps, and set of questions for each stage that you can use to kick start your own adventure.

The Hero's Map of Achievement doesn't give us detailed directions for our particular journey. Instead it explains the pattern for all types of change. Like any map, *The Hero's Map of Achievement* can be used at the start of the journey to plan the route, but it can also be used in the middle of the journey to help us figure out where we are and discover the next step forward. The map doesn't give us all the answers. It gives us all the questions. We discover the answers as we take the journey.

This simple map for change gives us a new way to take charge of any kind of change—from losing weight to gaining a relationship, from beating an addiction to beating the opposition, from running a business to running for president, from planning financial growth to planning spiritual growth, from getting rich to getting married to getting a life.

> *A car's headlights illuminate only a few yards into the darkness ahead, but you can complete the whole journey that way.*
> *– Steven Covey*

Anyone can understand *The Hero's Map of Achievement*. It's not intellectual or complex, but it is universal and profound. It is not highbrow or religious, but it is deep and wise.

Working Heroes

We think of heroes as amazing people like astronauts, Olympic athletes or celebrities. This isn't true. Heroes are not extraordinary people. They are ordinary people who do extraordinary things.

When prisoners in resettlement programmes or young people in drugs rehab take action to re-build their broken lives, they've done something extraordinary. When a failing business manager decides to take charge of change and turn his business around for good he's done something extraordinary. When an ordinary couple decide to re-build their marriage they set out on an extraordinary quest that promises lots of risk, hard work and a great reward. Whenever ordinary people step out on their own adventure of achievement they become ordinary heroes.

Work is the most ordinary thing we do. It's possible to apply the *Hero's Map of Achievement* in the workplace with great results. Susan is a good example of an Ordinary Hero at Work. A personnel manager in her thirties, Susan worked for an established, but uncreative company that produced car parts. She knew the challenges facing the company and wanted her people to accept the challenge of change with creativity and vision. But the workforce was complacent and slow to change. She could see they were plagued with fear of the future, low morale, high staff turnover and disappointing levels of production.

Underneath all that, Susan saw the positive capabilities of her fellow workers. After she experienced Ordinary Hero at Work Susan took a risk. She used some of her training budget to train her key people in the

Change your perception and you change your world

Ordinary Hero programme, and she bought copies of *How to Be an Ordinary Hero* for everyone in the company.

Almost overnight the whole company had a new way of seeing the challenges they faced. They shared a new vocabulary for change. They integrated the Ordinary Hero programme into their workplace, and productivity began to make an upturn. Employees saw their work problems and their personal challenges from a new perspective. They started to see opportunities, not obstacles. Work had become an adventure, and together the whole company became an ordinary hero.

This book is written to help you, your family, your workmates and your company become Ordinary Heroes.

Through the story of the magic key it provides a simple map for the journey: a map that is rooted in the wisest, simplest, most powerful stories of humanity.

The heros of all time have gone before us; the labyrinth is thoroughly known; we only have to follow the thread of the hero path.
— Joseph Campbell

Underlying this simple story is the sure belief that no matter what our circumstances, we can take charge of change. We can become all that we were created to be. We have been given the power to change ourselves, change our families, change our companies and therefore change our world. This is what life is for, and we do this by hearing the call and setting out on our own unique hero's quest.

I hope the hero's journey comes alive for you as it has for me. I don't think I've arrived. I'm still on the journey myself. I hope this book will help you — wherever you happen to be on your own quest. If you haven't

We shall not cease from exploration.
— T. S. Eliot

yet started out, don't be afraid. You can take charge of change. You can achieve your goals. You can become an Ordinary Hero. The adventure starts here.

How to Use This Book

■ Each of the ten chapters of *The Magic Key* are built around one stage in the *Hero's Map of Achievement* ©

■ On first reading don't worry too much about the ten stages. Just read *The Magic Key* and enjoy it as a story.

■ *The Ordinary Hero Workbook* explains more about each stage of the journey, and gives you questions that help you apply *The Hero's Map of Achievement* © to the challenge of change.

■ Use the questions to manage any kind of change: change at work, change in your family, change in your personal life.

■ *The Hero's Map of Achievement* © is a powerful tool that transforms lives! Pass the book on to a colleague, family member or friend, and buy several more to share.

■ Inside the back cover is a list of resources that will help you use *The Hero's Map of Achievement* © for personal growth, business success and better relationships.

How to Use This Book

The Magic Key

Chapter One – The Ordinary World

 Once upon a time, in a village called Over Wondring, there lived a young lad named Harry Dashwood. Harry was tall, bright and handsome. Harry had pizzazz. He had wavy dark hair, brown eyes and a smile that dazzled everyone. All the people in the village were convinced that Harry had it made. That's what everyone thought, but they didn't know Harry's secret.

Harry lived in a cottage on the edge of the village with Marion Doright, a kind, but strict old woman who everybody called 'Sarge'. Marion was upright, good and strong. She always knew the right thing to do. If anybody in the village had a problem, Sarge would be there with sensible advice, a 'to do' list and the right way to get the job done. Marion was an agony aunt, drill sergeant, Mother Superior, nanny, dog trainer, matchmaker and school mistress all wrapped up in one.

Behind the cottage was an ancient dark forest. In front was the road that led to the village. Down the lane was the farm where Harry worked. The farmer was a wiry old timer named Tom Doubtfire. Tom was as thin as a crane, with a long neck and a bald head that he always kept covered with a battered tweed hat. He had a habit of chewing slowly on a toothpick he kept in the corner of his mouth while he surveyed the world around him. Old Doubtfire was slow to speak and slow to smile; squinty-eyed and shrewd. He was a good judge of character, and naturally liked people, even if he wondered what they were after. "Can't be too careful" was one of his mottoes, and although his farmhouse was falling down and he dressed in shabby old clothes, everybody reckoned he was far richer than he ever let on.

Harry was happy living with Sarge in Over Wondring. The thatched cottage was cosy and Marion loved Harry and looked after his every need like clockwork. He liked working for Farmer Tom, who was always fair and faithful. Harry did a whole range of jobs around the farm. He had a sharp and able mind and liked solving problems quickly. Marion and Farmer Tom liked Harry, but they didn't know his secret.

Harry's best friend was an easygoing cook who worked at The Dancing Donkey — the local inn. His name was Marvin Makepeace, and like many cooks, Marvin enjoyed not only making good food, but sampling the result. He had a head of curly brown hair, a large belly and a large circle of friends, and he liked nothing better than relaxing with them after work, sharing stories and tall tales. If anyone asked if a glass of beer was half full or half empty, Marvin would drain the glass and answer, 'Neither.' Harry liked Marvin because he knew how to take it easy and chill out and Marvin liked Harry because he always had some new and exciting project. Marvin was his best friend, but he didn't know Harry's secret either

Most days Harry woke up early and worked through a list of chores Sarge had set him. While he did that she'd cook him a good breakfast, and send him off with a lunch box crammed full of home made goodies. After a busy day and supper, he'd help Sarge wash the dishes, then have a wash, shave, splash his face with cologne, brush back his shock of brown hair, put on a smart clean shirt and head down to the Dancing Donkey for the rest of the evening. His friends were always glad to see him—especially Ginny Martin—the mayor's daughter.

Ginny didn't know Harry's secret either, and the secret was this: beneath the dazzling surface, Harry was miserable. He felt miserable that he felt miserable. On the outside everything was bright. On the inside everything was dark. Everybody in the village thought Harry was happy and successful. He knew that he was an unhappy failure. What made matters worse was that his friends all seemed perfectly happy with their lot. Harry didn't like to criticise them, but sometimes their viewpoint was a bit small. They never seemed to think of anything outside the village or their ordinary lives. Because of this Harry felt lonely, confused and frustrated. He didn't really connect with anyone. He was restless. Something was missing. Was this all there was to life? Shouldn't there be more? Harry didn't know more of *what*, just more.

When things got bad Harry also wondered who his parents were and what had happened to them. Sarge only ever referred to it as 'the disaster'. Whenever Harry asked, she said he would discover the whole story soon enough. All she told him was that his parents died in a terrible accident when he was a baby, and that, of his whole family, only he was left. She was his nurse when the disaster happened, and she had bundled him away in the darkest part of the night and brought him here to live in safety. When he asked Marion if he might try to find his family she looked at him long and hard, then smiled sadly and said, "Nothing happens, but first a dream."

Sometimes when he was working at a boring job Harry would dream of a different kind of life. If he was riding on the cart behind the old workhorse he would imagine that he was a prince wearing rich robes and driving a red two seater carriage with silver wheels, pulled by a team of white stallions. Sometimes on his walks home from the Dancing Donkey Harry would imagine that he had a beautiful princess on his arm—a woman who was sweet, intelligent, beautiful and kind — a woman who was as hard as diamonds and soft as moonlight.

When he was chopping wood or swinging a scythe Harry would see himself as a dashing knight wielding a lance and bright sword. When he was trying to solve a problem he would see himself as a grave and quiet king in his throne room with queues of people waiting for his wise advice.

Eventually Harry's dreams began to occupy more and more of his time. He started to imagine how he might get a red carriage with six white horses. He wondered where he might meet women more beautiful and clever than the girls in Over Wondring. He asked himself where he might take sword lessons or learn to shoot the crossbow, or where he might acquire the wisdom to answer all the riddles in the world. He also wondered about his family, and if any of them were still alive.

Harry didn't dare tell Tom Doubtfire about his dreams. He would have scowled, clipped Harry around the ear and told him not to be daft. Once Harry confided in Marvin, telling him all the great things he would do one day, but Marvin just went quiet and said, 'I don't know what you're talking about. Our life in Over Wondring is good. Why do you want to make yourself so unhappy by dreaming about what you can't be?"

Harry flashed his dazzling smile and said, "You're a good friend Marvin. I suppose you're right. I should get on with things and stop complaining. I just keep thinking there's more.

Marvin thought for a moment, 'Maybe your being so restless is a sign that you should move on.'

'I think you're right,' Harry replied, 'You know what Sarge always says, 'Ask and you will receive. Seek and you shall find. Knock and the door will be opened.'"

Poor Harry; the more he dreamed, the more miserable he became. His daydreams eventually invaded his night dreams. One night he dreamed that he was a prince in silver armour, that he had climbed a mountain clutching a large golden key. He dreamed of cliffs and chasms and dragons and a tall tower standing at the peak of a high mountain. He felt frustrated as he looked up at the tower. In his dream he knew the tower held some great treasure. He looked around for an answer, then saw that through all the adventures he had always held tight to the golden key.

Suddenly he saw himself standing on top of the mountain with the tower reduced to rubble at his feet. He felt fantastic. He had overcome all things, and to prove his point he planted a banner on top of the mountain as a sign of his victory. Then he realised he had dropped the key over the edge. He leaned over and saw it fall down and disappear into the darkness.

Then he woke up. In the darkness the Sarge's words echoed in his mind, "Nothing happens but first a dream" She'd said, and "Ask and you shall receive. Seek and you shall find."

Harry went back to sleep, and the next morning was late getting up. The first thing he did was scribble down the Sarge's words in a little notebook, and then he quickly pulled on his clothes. He couldn't find his boots anywhere. Finally he sat still and tried to remember where they might be. He got down and looked under the bed. The boots weren't there, but in the darkness at the back he spotted something. It was shining in the dark. He clambered under the bed, sneezed in the dust and reached into the darkness for the curious object. He crawled out from under the bed and squinted as a sudden shaft of light came in through the window. In his hand was a large golden key. It was exactly like the one he had seen in his dream.

Harry's Journal

- Nothing happens, but first a dream
- Your restlessness is telling you to move on.
- Ask and you shall receive. Seek and you shall find.

Chapter Two – Hearing the Call

As he held the key, Harry heard a faint humming sound from outside the window. He squinted into the bright sunlight and blinked. For a moment he saw blue spots in front of his eyes, then, as the hum got louder, the blue spots whirled and turned, then came together into one blue circle. As he watched, the blue circle grew larger. He saw a woman's face in the circle, then as the circle grew even bigger it filled with the figure of a plump, black woman in a long, blue dress. He heard her faint voice calling out, "Hang on there! I'm just coming into focus!"

Finally the shimmering blue circle disappeared and he saw the woman clearly. She was just eighteen inches tall, and she was standing on the windowsill. Her flowing blue dress was alive with a large floral pattern. Her grey hair was pulled back in an untidy bun at the nape of her neck. She wore half glasses low on her nose and was rummaging around in a large blue handbag.

"Who are you? Harry gasped.

The woman looked up. "Oh, I have lots of names. Some people call me the Oracle. Others call me Gabriel." She smiled kindly, "but you can call me Gloria Goodbody. I'm your Fairy Godmother." Then she began rummaging in the bag again.

"Fairy Godmother?!' said Harry. ' I thought they only existed in fairy tales!"

The little woman pulled out a packet of mints, and sat down on the edge of the windowsill with an exhausted sigh, popped one into her mouth and frowned at Harry, "This *is* a fairy tale. Did you forget?"

"What do you want?" Harry asked.

"That's what I was just about to ask you," said the fairy Godmother.

Harry's eyes lit up, "Alright then, I want a red carriage with silver wheels and six white horses…"

"I know. I know," said Gloria wearily, "and you want to be rich and marry a beautiful princess, and you want to be a great warrior and a wise king…"

Harry was shocked, "But how did you know that? Is it magic?"

"Of course not. That's what all men think they want. But what do you *really* want? "

"I really want a red carriage with…"

Gloria rolled her eyes, "Puleeze! I'm a busy woman." She checked her watch, then tapped it and frowned at Harry. "Listen son, you're an emergency visit. Because you found that key, I've had to squeeze you in between an old woman who just about got eaten by a wolf and yet another house maid who wants to go to the palace ball." She rolled her eyes, "The pressures on a fairy godmother! You wouldn't believe it."

Harry sat down on the bed holding the key. He felt totally confused. He glanced down at the key, then stared at the blue fairy.

"Did I ask for too much?"

Gloria smiled and said, "No, honey, you asked for too little." She kept smiling at him. Waiting.

Harry felt awkward and blurted out, "Why did I find this key? What does it mean?"

Gloria chuckled, "I'm not here to give you answers. I'm here to give you the questions. Find a magic key and something magical happens to you. The key will unlock your destiny."

"But what is my destiny?!" Harry cried.

Gloria shrugged, "Good question." Then she leaned forward and squinted at him, "In fact, it's the only question." She looked around the room then turned to Harry. "It's all very cosy here, but you didn't honestly think you were going to spend the rest of your days holed up with Sarge did you?"

"But what am I supposed to do?"

"Follow your bliss."

"My *what?*"

"Your bliss. What you really want. Your dreams. You've been dreaming haven't you? Dreaming of something better?"

Harry nodded.

"That's why you found the key. Your dreams led you to it." She paused as Harry took it in. "So you've got some dreams." She continued, "That's very nice, but dreams are cheap. Anybody can have a dream. They're penny a pound."

Harry hung his head, "I guess my dreams were just ridiculous."

"Nonsense! The dreams are important. The dreams are good, but dreams on their own are just piffle. You have to move from the dream to figure out what you really want."

"But I don't know what I really want!"

"True enough. It's easier to get what you think you want than know what you really want."

"What's that supposed to mean?"

Gloria smiled, "Go figure. Here's a hint. To find out what you really want, ask what you would do if you were not afraid."

"Shall I do that now?"

Gloria pulled herself up to her full foot and a half and looked severely at Harry. "Of course not. It's a very personal thing. Do it later, then when you've figured out what you really want, you have to decide who is going to make it happen." She looked hard at Harry. "Who do you think is going to give you what you want?"

There was a long silence, then Harry looked at her hopefully, "You?"

Gloria threw back her head and laughed, "Guess again! It's you."

"Me?"

"Yes." Gloria shook her finger at him and said, "You. You. You, and nobody else but you."

"But…"

"No ifs ands and buts about it. It's you, and the sooner you get it out of your head that me or Sarge, or a genie in a bottle is going to give you your heart's desire the better. You've got to do it, or its not worth doodly squat. You choose. You're either the victim of your fate or the master of your destiny."

"Aren't you even going to help?"

Gloria reached into her bag and pulled out a wand and tapped him on the nose. "What do you think I've been doing so far? Now listen closely."

Harry leaned forward.

"What you've just discovered is the key to your destiny."

Harry held up the golden key. "You mean this?"

"Yes and no." the blue fairy reached for the key and touched it with her wand. It began to glow, and as it started to glow Harry felt all tingly. He shivered and then felt warm from the inside out. As the warmth spread through his body he started to stand up more straight and tall. He took a deep breath. It was like a wave of energy swept through him from head to toe. Suddenly he felt a surge of confidence. He was in charge! Nobody else. He felt like he'd made a real decision for the first time, and the awareness was like waking up from a long sleep. He blinked and grinned at Gloria, filled with a sense of new power and determination.

Gloria stared at him for a moment, then smiled with approval and put the wand back into her bag and stood up. Suddenly there was a low buzzing sound like an alarm clock going off and in a puff of blue smoke Gloria vanished.

Harry gasped, blinked and stared at the windowsill, then looked around the room. There was a hazy patch of shimmering blue light spinning and flitting about the room. Then he heard Gloria's voice. It was faint and fading fast, "I forgot to say that there's a lost treasure that somebody better find pretty soon…and don't forget the princess… The key will unlock the door… oh dear, I'm losing focus …I expect you'll find the way…Good luck m'dear." And then she and her voice were gone.

Harry looked around the room. The blue glow had faded into the bright sky of morning. It was a day like any other day, except that he was still holding the magic key, and he hadn't figured out what the key was for. In fact the only thing he had got from Gloria's visit was more questions than answers.

He trotted downstairs for breakfast, careful to hide the key in his rucksack. Over breakfast he asked Sarge, "Let's say you really wanted something and decided to do everything you could to get it. What would you do first?"

Marion stood with a fry pan in her hand and gazed at Harry. She dished up his breakfast, wiped her hands and sat at the table opposite him.

After a long pause for thought she said, "I don't suppose you want to tell me what it is?"

Harry shook his head, "Sorry, but I'm not really sure myself yet."

"I see. First I'd take time to figure out what it is I really wanted."

Harry nodded and shovelled a mouthful of scrambled egg into his mouth.

"Once I'd decided, I'd write the dream down. But dreams are unrealistic, so I would try to turn the dream into a vision. Here's an example: I once dreamt of running a school for fine pupils who would grow up to change the world. From that I got the vision of being a nanny. A vision is something possible that grows from the dream…be realistic, but not pessimistic."

"Then I'd set some goals. Write them down. Make it real. Give yourself long term goals. Where will you be ten years from now? Give yourself mid term goals. Where will you be five years from now? Give yourself short term goals. Where will you be two years from now? Where will you be next month? Write it down. Visualise it. Make it real. Make it so real in your imagination that you can taste it." She smiled proudly. "My father taught me that; and it's never failed. Can you do that?"

"I can try."

"Don't try. Do or don't do. Finally, pin down some actions. These are things you're going to do today. Actions you can do that don't rely on anyone else for their success. Decide what they are, make a list and then cross them off the list as you do them."

"Now hurry up with your breakfast, you'll be late for work and Farmer Tom will have you cleaning out the stables."

Harry put his lunchbox in the rucksack and spotted the key. As he hurried down the road Harry knew what he really wanted. He wanted to find that treasure. If he were rich he could do anything. If he were rich he could have that red two seater carriage he dreamt about. If he were rich he might even marry a princess and fulfil his dream of being a prince. He stopped and pulled his journal out of his rucksack and scribbled down what he'd learned that day, then shoved it back into the backpack and hurried on his way.

As he approached the farmyard he saw Tom Doubtfire leaning on the gate waiting for him.

"Ah, there you are young Master Harry," he called, "head in the clouds again when you ought to be here working? Now hurry up. I've got some stables that need mucking out."

Harry's Journal

- What would you do if you were not afraid?
- You're either a victim of your fate or the master of your destiny
- Turn Dreams into Visions, Visions into Goals and Goals into action.

Chapter Three – Refusing the Call

 Harry suddenly decided that cleaning out the stables was the last thing he wanted to do that day. His rucksack was packed with a huge lunch. He had the golden key. Gloria Goodbody had told him to go find the treasure. Sarge had encouraged him to follow his dream.

Suddenly all his unhappiness and dreams came together, and like a volcano, it burst from him. He ran up to Tom Doubtfire and burst out, "I can't work for you today!"

"What do you mean you can't work today?" blurted the farmer. "Are you sick or are you mad?"

How could Harry say what was in his heart? How could he say, "I have to find my destiny! I'm going to be rich. I'm going to be a prince!" It would sound foolish. Farmer Doubtfire had no children, and more than once he had told Harry that he would inherit the farm. How could Harry say, "I don't want a farm, I want to find the treasure. I want to be a prince, not a farmer."? It was impossible. So Harry tried to look sickly and replied, "Yes, I'm not feeling well. I have to go home to bed."

The old farmer squinted at Harry, studying him for what

seemed ages. "Alright then, but you'd better be here first thing in the morning, and don't you be getting any ideas above your station!"

Harry turned toward home, but he looked over his shoulder, and as soon as the old farmer went into the house Harry ran past the farm, over the hill and down the road toward town. He felt a thrill of excitement flood through him. The adventure had started! He remembered something Sarge used to say, "Life is a daring adventure or nothing at all."

He stopped for a moment and sat down under a large tree. He dug his journal out of his rucksack and set down his vision. Crazy as it might sound, he knew that he was supposed to be a prince. To do that he had to find the treasure. Gloria Goodbody had said something about a princess... it had happened before, that a princess fell in love with a commoner and married him, so he set that down as his vision—to marry a princess, and rule over his own country with her as queen.

The blue fairy said that the key was connected with his dream, so he scribbled down that his long term goal was to use the key to find the treasure. His mid term goal was to find out the meaning of the key and how to use it. All of this only raised more questions, so Harry wrote down that his short term goal was to find someone who could answer his questions. His first action; the thing he could do today without depending on anybody else was clear: In order to find the person who could help he had to leave Over Wandring.

He shoved the journal back into the rucksack, shrugged

it on to his back and headed away from the farm towards town.

In the town square Harry spotted his friend Marvin. Marvin was in his chef's uniform, heading for the Dancing Donkey.

Marvin waved and called, "Harry! What are you doing here in town? Shouldn't you be out on the farm?"

Harry ran over and grabbed Marvin by the arm. "Marvin. It's happened!"

"What's happened?"

"I've found the magic key. A fairy godmother has told me to seek my destiny! I'm leaving Over Wandring for good!"

Marvin frowned and said, "But where are you going?"

"I don't know yet."

"What are you going to do?"

"I don't know yet."

"Have you got any money?"

"Not much."

"Why do you want to leave?"

Harry hung his head, "You'll laugh at me."

"No I won't. Tell me," insisted Marvin.

Harry looked at his friend and said, "I am going to be a prince—not a farmer. I need to start now or I'll never succeed."

Marvin didn't laugh. He looked away for a time, then looked back to his friend and shook his head, "Harry, listen to some sense. You don't know anyone outside the village. You don't have any money. The only way for you to be a prince is to marry a princess, and they only marry rich men."

"I'll find the treasure first!"

Marvin looked at him for a moment, then said, "You'll never do that. You're dreaming. What about Farmer Doubtfire? He's depending on you to take over the farm. Your chances here are fantastic! Think of others; what about Sarge? Who's going to look after her in her old age? You can't just walk out."

Harry was angry, but he had to admit that Marvin had a point. Where did he get such an idea that he would ever find treasure or that he would someday be a prince? He didn't have any experience except on the farm. How would he go about it? Where would he go? Maybe he'd dreamt it all. Maybe the fairy godmother was just his imagination. Maybe he was going mad. He was just a dreamer. He was a superficial and proud fool. Already he was feeling hungry. Once his lunch was gone what would he eat? Where would he sleep?

"You're right Marvin. I guess I was just getting carried away."

Marvin draped his arm over Harry's shoulder, "There. Don't be discouraged. You just need a day off. Why don't you go for a nice long walk in the woods, head back to Sarge for your supper, then come down to the Dancing Donkey this evening and have a game of cards with me and Ginny and all your friends?"

Marvin got up and said, "I've got to get to work! You can be sure your secret is safe with me. See you tonight!"

Harry sat on the bench for what seemed ages, then stood up and plodded back up the hill towards home. It had been a short lived adventure. He didn't have what was necessary for the journey. He didn't have the money or knowledge. Everyone he knew was against the idea or would be if they knew about it. Worst of all, Harry wasn't sure he had what it takes for such an adventure. There were too many doubts and fears and questions still bubbling away in his mind.

As Harry walked up the hill he wrestled with the problems and questions. He blamed himself. He was stupid to have ever thought he could go on such an adventure and become a prince. On the other hand, maybe it was a good thing that he had questions, doubts and fears. He suddenly remembered something Farmer Doubtfire had said when he first started working at the farm. One day he couldn't figure out now to mend a piece of machinery and Farmer Doubtfire had said, "If you think you can't or think you can, you're probably right." Harry smiled as he remembered how long it had taken him to figure out that riddle. Another time he was worried that he was pestering the farmer with too many questions, and he'd muttered gruffly, "Don't be afraid of questions. Questions lead to answers."

He sat down for a rest under the same tree on the way home as he had on the way into town. He got his lunch out and munched his way through it. As he did he got out the magic key and held it in one hand as he ate. It gave him a good feeling to hold the key, and as he ate his lunch he began to feel better about his adventure. Maybe he would try again another day.

The sun was warm on his face, and Harry fell asleep under the tree. When he woke up he realised that he had dropped the magic key. He looked all around on the ground, but couldn't find it anywhere. Then he heard a loud bird call and looked up. High above him, in the middle of the tree sat a large bright red parrot with yellow markings and what looked like a huge beak. Then Harry looked again. In the bird's beak was the magic key.

The bird watched him curiously for a moment, then Harry gasped in horror as the bird, with the key in her beak, took off from the branch and flew into the dark forest.

Harry's Journal

- Life is a daring adventure or nothing at all.
- Whether you think you can or think you can't, you're probably right.
- Don't be afraid of questions. Questions lead to answers.

Chapter Four – Meeting the Mentor

Before he thought twice about it, Harry jumped up and followed the bird into the forest. At first the red and yellow parrot was high up in the trees, chattering and calling in a musical way low in her throat. As she flew from tree to tree Harry followed. He noticed that the further he went into the forest, the more the bird came down closer to him. Finally the parrot was at eye level on a branch just in front of Harry. She still held the key in her beak, and whenever Harry reached for the key she chattered and flapped and jumped to a branch just beyond his reach.

Exasperated, Harry stopped and looked around. This part of the forest was ancient, dark and deep. The gnarled trees seemed to be watching him and waiting for some great thing to happen, as if Harry had an important choice to make. Harry pressed further into the wood, and the further he went the thicker the brambles and ivy became. Far above, the sunlight filtered through the canopy of leaves. The darker it became, and the thicker the forest, the more Harry began to think that he'd made a mistake. How would he ever find his way home?

Then, just as he was about to turn around, the red bird appeared again, then circled and flew up to perch on a branch high above and in front of him. Harry followed, pushing through a screen of bushes and found himself in a small clearing. On the other side of the clearing, built in and around an ancient oak was a tiny, crooked thatched house. He looked again—it was more of a hut than a cottage. The thatch was tattered and had moss and weeds growing out of it. A chimney leaned crazily to one side, with smoke leaking out of crumbling brickwork, and Harry noticed that the green front door was ajar. The red bird hopped along the ground with Harry's key still firmly in her beak, then flapped up and flew through the door into the cottage.

Harry approached the open door warily and peeked inside. The single room of the cottage was crammed full of a whole range of extraordinary junk. A large table dominated the centre of the room. One leg was broken and propped up on a pile of books. The table held a pile of filthy dishes, strange glass tubes and bottles. Model flying machines hung from the ceiling and there were mountains of books with papers sticking out piled everywhere. The walls were lined floor to ceiling with bookshelves that were heaving with leather bound volumes, stuffed animals, half eaten plates of food, carved figures that were half human, half beast and a whole range of mugs with people's faces carved on them. The fire was blazing happily, and in front of the fire was a large wing backed chair. From the doorway Harry saw two long legs stretched out from the chair towards the fire. The thin legs were covered with green and black striped knee socks, and the feet were stuck into a pair of red velvet slippers.

"Hello?" Harry ventured.

No reply.

"Hello?" he said a bit more loudly.

A tall, gangly old man with a long white beard sprang up from the chair. As he did so he dropped a book with a thud on his foot, hopped around in pain and looked around for the source of the interruption, and then spotted Harry.

"Harry smiled politely, "Sorry to disturb you, but could I have my key back please?"

The old man was wearing a deep yellow robe like a quilted dressing gown that went to the floor. The robe was patterned with nine different types of dark blue stars. The old man looked at Harry and blinked. "Who are you? And what do you mean by asking for a key?"

Harry began to explain, then the old man looked over to the red bird, who sat perfectly still on her perch with the key in her beak.

"Ahh!" said the old man. "That explains everything! Come in. Come in. I've been waiting for you."

"You have?" said Harry.

"Indeed I have. My name is Dominus Maginot, but most people call me Father Maginot."

"Father Maginot! Harry exclaimed, "the famous wizard! I thought you were just the stuff of children's stories."

The old man chuckled, "But I am! I *am* the stuff of children's stories. Children of all ages keep me in their dreams!"

Harry frowned and said, "I think your red bird stole my key and led me here."

"That's exactly what she did!" Maginot exclaimed. "Isn't she clever?" He leaned forward. "We've been looking for the bearer of that key for a very long time and here you are at last!"

"But.." said Harry. "What does it all mean?"

Maginot led him over to the fire, pulled up a stool and pushed Harry on to it. He looked at Harry for a long time, then beamed at him, clearly delighted. Finally he said, "My boy, you will bear the key to the stone tower, defeat the evil Baron Blackforze, discover the treasure and bear it home for all of us."

"What!" said Harry? "I thought this was about *my* treasure! I thought there was a princess involved, and nobody told me about an evil Baron."

Maginot got up, crossed the room and rummaged around in a cupboard, all the time muttering, and humming to himself.

Finally he pulled out a small package, returned to his chair and said, "Yes, I'm sure a princess does come into it somewhere along the way, but for the life of me, I can't tell you the details. You'll have to figure that out yourself." He looked long and hard at Harry then said, "The main thing is to realise that you have done everything right so far. I know about your doubts and fears my boy, but no adventurer ever got anywhere without doubts and fears. They're part of the journey, and only a fool would set out with no doubts or fears."

"I'm afraid I don't know the way. Can you help?"

The old magician smiled and lifted the packet he'd got

from the cupboard and handed it to Harry. "Of course! Ask and you shall receive."

Harry unwrapped the package. Inside a cloth wrapping he found a brown, folded piece of leather. Harry unfolded it four times until it lay on top of the table. It was a map — an old fashioned, hand drawn map with roads and pictures and sailing ships and dragons. As Harry looked at it his eyes seemed to go out of focus, then he saw that if he stared at the map long enough ten little pictures appeared within it.

"It's a magic map! " Harry said.

Maginot was glowing with pride, "I made it myself many years ago when I went on a similar journey. An adventure, like all work, needs instruction and tools. The map is a tool for your journey. The pictures will show you the way." He reached into a large canvas bag, "Here is something else!"

Harry took a small, oval flat object that was wrapped in paper. He unwrapped it. "A mirror?" he said.

The magician looked grave, "A magic mirror. Not only do you see your face, but you see your inner self." He paused for impact and said, "You see not only what you do and think, but why you do and think those things. You will find it most helpful on the journey."

Harry turned to the magician, "But where am I going? What am I supposed to do?"

Maginot looked at him deeply, "I thought you already decided that. Something about treasure of some sort?... a princess? That seems right to me."

"But…where? What?…"

"Come, come" said the magician, you know where you're going, you just don't know how to get there, but do you expect to know the road before you've travelled on it?"

"I suppose not."

"When you travel in a coach at night the headlamps shine only a few yards ahead, but you can complete the whole journey that way." The old man stroked his beard and smiled at Harry, "You want success, but you also want it quickly without much effort don't you?"

Harry frowned. The magician seemed to understand everything about him.

Maginot stood tall and put one finger in the air. "Inspiration. Preparation. Perspiration. Then success."

Harry nodded and repeated, "Inspiration. Preparation. Perspiration. Then Success."

"In that order," the magician smiled, "but unfortunately, not in equal proportions…Now I have just one thing to tell you. The key has an inscription on it." The parrot gave him the key and he put it into a jar of green liquid. It sizzled and hissed and green smoke poured from the jar, then the magician took tweezers and lifted the key and gave it to Harry.

Sure enough, inscribed on the shaft of the key were strange words. "It's a foreign language. I can't read it!

"I expect you will find someone who can," said Maginot as he rummaged in a pile of boots, walking sticks and suitcases. Eventually he surfaced with a larger rucksack. As he emptied it out he waved toward the back of the house. "You'll find plenty of food for the journey back there. Help yourself to whatever you like."

"Aren't you coming with me?" Harry asked.

Maginot stared at Harry solemnly, then shook his head, "I'm afraid not. The hero steps out on a solitary path. I can show you the path, but only you can walk in it." Are you willing?"

Harry pondered the question for a moment. As he did he clutched the key tightly, and felt a sudden strength.

At that moment the window of the cottage blew open with a crash and Harry watched as the red bird squawked twice and flew from her perch and out into the forest.

Harry's Journal

- The mentor informs, affirms, and terrifies.
- Learn to Live, Live to Learn.
- Inspiration, Preparation, Perspiration. Then success.

Chapter Five – Crossing the Threshold

Father Maginot laughed, "She's anxious to make a start."

"Does she understand what we say?" Harry asked.

"She does more than understand what we say!" the wizard went to the window and called, "Don't you Scarlett?".

"Whatever you say greybeard." the bird squawked as she fluttered back and sat on the windowsill.

"She can talk!" Harry exclaimed.

"Of course I can talk! What did you think? I'm a parrot!"

"Unfortunately, she talks more than she thinks," said Maginot. "Come now, let's get ready." He helped Harry load his rucksack full of food, the map and the mirror. He took the magic key from Harry, rummaged around in an old box and came up with a golden chain. He threaded the chain through the key and placed it over Harry's neck, chuckling to himself, "The keys to the kingdom!"

Maginot gave Harry a flask of water from the well, added a walking stick and a loop of strong rope, then stepped back and smiled at Harry. "You'll need to set off through the forest. That's the quickest way to the upward road."

"Shouldn't I go back to say good-bye to Sarge?"

Maginot looked grave, "No turning back. From now on it's 'fare forward voyager!' Come along." With that he took Harry's arm and led him out the door and across the clearing to where a small path led through the forest. "I'll go with you as far as the edge, and from there you're on your own."

Maginot led Harry at a brisk pace down a hill, across a shallow wooded valley and further into the darkest part of the forest. Scarlett followed them, flying from tree to tree, then finally flew down and settled on Harry's shoulder, "I like it!" she squawked, "An adventure! I haven't been on a real quest for ages. Old long beard there does nothing but sit at home with his nose stuck in a book. Booooring. That's what he is. Give me the fresh air and open road anytime!" Scarlett started singing in a loud screech, "I love to go a –wandering, along the mountain track, and as I go, I love to sing…"

Maginot gave the bird a dark look and moaned, "Spare us the boy scout songs red bird. You think I'm dull, but what you need is to settle down and learn how to finish a good book, or for that matter, finish anything. You're far too flighty for your own good."

"Flighty!" Scarlett said, "Flighty! I like that. What does he expect? I'm a bird for crying out loud!"

Harry stopped laughing as they turned a corner and started to climb a steep path upward. Suddenly Maginot halted so abruptly that Harry ran into him and Scarlett fell off his shoulder and flapped to the ground.

"Hey Longbeard!" the bird squawked, "Why the emergency stop?"

Maginot grabbed the bird's beak. "Shut up you fool! There's someone following us."

Harry looked back into the dark forest, but didn't see or hear anything. "Is it dangerous?" he asked.

"Of course its dangerous!" Maginot whispered. "Did you think a quest would be safe?" He looked around carefully, then led onward. At last they came to the top of the hill and Maginot stopped. They were at the edge of a steep cliff. In the distance a wide green plain opened out with purple peaked mountains beyond. Through the middle of the plain a wide river snaked downward to the sea. In the centre of the distant range of mountains Harry saw a rocky peak with a single tall tower on the summit. Like a tiny red thread a brick-cobbled road could be seen weaving across the plain to a bridge across the river and then to the mountains beyond.

"Your first step is down that cliff face. It's a short cut to the brick road which leads across the valley and upward to the mountain." Maginot said. "The tower is the lookout station for Baron Blackforze's fortress."

"Down the cliff face! But I've never..."

"You've never abseiled down a cliff face? You've never ridden a horse, or been challenged to a duel or fought for your life with a terrible villain? You've never kissed a fair maiden? You've never taken a risk or stepped out not knowing where the road would lead? Did you think finding the treasure and the princess was all about sitting at home by the fire and sleeping in your featherbed each night? Did you think someone would deliver success to you on a silver platter? Did you imagine the quest was all about doing the same thing you've always done, just a bit differently?"

Maginot shook his head, "No, no, my boy, if you do what you've always done you'll get what you've always got. A quest is about doing what you've never done before and getting far more than you thought possible. The quest is about stepping into a world far more beautiful and terrible than you could ever imagine."

The sun had ducked behind a cloud and a cold wind started to whip around them. Father Maginot seemed impatient and glanced around nervously. Harry looked over the cliff edge. It fell away in a sheer drop for about fifty feet, ending in scrubby bushes. Beyond the bushes he could see nothing. "Beyond those bushes it drops into mid air!"

"Indeed it might." Maginot said.

"Do you know what's down there?"

Maginot shook his head. "It's all changed since I passed by here last."

Harry turned to go back through the forest, "There must be some other way."

"There is no other way." Maginot said. "Do you want to go on this quest or not?"

Harry shouted in panic, "Yes, I do! I want to go, but I don't know how!"

At that moment there was a crashing from further down the hill. Something was coming up through the underbrush in their direction. Harry turned to look for Maginot, but he had stepped out of the path. Scarlett started squawking in fear, "Watch out Harry Houdini, something's coming! Get your stick handy. It could be a lion, a tiger or a bear!"

Harry turned again and looked over the edge. Behind him a wild animal was racing up the hill. In front was the cliff edge. There was no place to hide; no place to run. He turned desperately to Maginot for help, but he just crossed his arms and watched Harry.

"What shall I do?" Harry cried.

"Do what you must." The wizard said. "Jump!"

Harry turned away in frustration. The drop from the cliff was terrifying. The wind howled and pulled at him, making him waver on the edge. Brandishing his walking stick, he turned from the cliff to face the attacker. Suddenly a round figure burst through the bushes from the side, and floored him with a rugby tackle. "I've got you Harry! I won't let that magician turn you into a toad or anything un-natural!"

Marvin Makepeace and Harry rolled over, and before he could get a hand hold Harry found himself hurtling over the edge and down the cliff face. They crashed through the bushes below and tumbled head over heels for another fifty feet down a gravel embankment until they landed in a pile of leaves and moss at the bottom of the cliff.

Harry's Journal

- All glory comes from daring to begin
- If you don't risk anything you risk even more.
- Do what you must … Jump!

Chapter Six – Trials, Allies and Enemies

Harry sat up and moaned. He checked carefully and realised he'd got away with just a few bruises and scratches. He got up and brushed himself off. "Marvin! What are you doing here?"

"When you went missing I decided to come and find you." Marvin said. He sat up and beamed at Harry, "Good thing I saved you from that evil magician isn't it?"

Harry looked up the cliff. Father Maginot was gone. They'd never get back up that cliff without help from on top. Then he saw a little red shape circling down towards them. It was Scarlett. She flew down and perched on a branch, cast a beady eye on Harry and whistled, "When you decide to act, you don't mess around do you? That was the quickest way down a cliff I've ever seen! I like that. I think I'll come with you." Then she cocked her head and looked at Marvin, "Who's the fat guy?"

"Marvin," Harry said, as he offered his friend a hand up, "Meet Scarlett. It looks like we're in this together. There's no going back up that hill, and I intend to find that brick road I saw. Are you coming with me?"

Marvin frowned and thought about it for a moment, then broke into a grin, "Sure I am. You're going to need some friends on this journey, and I was getting tired of that old Dancing Donkey anyway."

"A Dancing Donkey!" Scarlett crowed, "Now that's something I'd love to see, a donkey that can dance! Take me to him!"

Harry and Marvin made their way down the hill and found themselves in a thick forest. They lost sight of the distant mountains, but Scarlett flew up and ahead as a scout, flying back every few moments with a new idea and a fresh perspective. Eventually they came to the bottom of a steep, rocky hill. As they stood at the bottom Scarlett said, "There's no way around it boys. The brick road is on the far side of the hill. The hill turns into a cliff face further along to the left, and to the right there's nothing but a huge swamp. You'll have to go up and over, and this is the best place."

Marvin sat down to rest while Harry surveyed the problem. "Ever climbed a mountain before?" Scarlett squawked. "What are you going to do?"

Marvin rummaged in Harry's rucksack, found an apple and shrugged, "I guess we'll find a way."

"I've got it!" Harry said as he pulled the rope off his shoulder, "Scarlett, fly to the top of the hill," then as he tied a knot in the end of the rope he said, "Lodge this knot in the fork of a tree, then we'll use the rope to climb up."

Harry went up first, then held the rope for Marvin to follow. Once on top they continued across a wide plateau, until the land started to drop away down the other side.

Before night fell they could see the distant mountains again, and in the stone tower they could see a tiny light in the single high window. They hurried downhill, and found a small cave to shelter in for the night. Marvin built a fire and cooked some bacon while Harry went to gather more wood and Scarlett went hunting for her own supper.

As the fire died down, the stars came out and a full moon began to glow softly in the night sky. Harry rolled out their blankets and found the little oval magic mirror in his ruck-sack. He pulled it out and put it between himself and Marvin.

"What's that?" Marvin asked,

"It's a magic mirror. Father Maginot, the old wizard, gave it to me."

"What does it do?"

"I'm not sure. He said it would show me not only what I wanted, but why I wanted it."

Marvin said, "I'm not sure I want to look into a mirror like that."

"Why not?"

"I might not like what I see."

Suddenly a deep voice from the mirror said, "What you see is always true. How you see it is what matters."

"That's Father Maginot's voice!" Harry cried.

Harry looked into the mirror and saw his face reflected, then as he stared harder his face began to change. He saw a fine gold crown appear on his head, and as he watched he felt a strange strong glow of confidence swell through him before the image faded.

"Marvin! You have to look into this mirror. I saw myself

with a crown on my head. It means I am going to be a prince one day."

Marvin frowned and moved over to the mirror cautiously. As he gazed into the mirror he saw his face. He was asleep with a faint smile on his face. Then as his face grew older, a white dove appeared and circled around his head. He woke up, reached up for it, held it in his hands for a moment, then released it and watched it fly away.

"What do you think that means?" Marvin asked.

"Harry laughed, "I don't know, ask the mirror.""

Before he could ask Father Maginot's voice came from the mirror, "Your name Marvin Makepeace is no mistake. The white dove is the sign of peace."

Before long Scarett had returned, found a perch on a ledge in the cave and settled with her head under her wing. Before the fire died Marvin and Harry's conversation had died and they were asleep on the first night of their adventure.

Their journey down the hill and across the broad woodland took seven days and seven nights. On the eighth day they came out of the woodland and found themselves on the brick road they had seen from the edge a whole week before.

"Father Maginot said this way would lead to the brick road." Harry said, "Now we're here, which way do we go?"

"Why don't you look at the map?" Marvin suggested

Harry grinned, "Why didn't I think of that?"

He dug out the map and saw the brick road come into focus. Marvin looked over his shoulder. They turned the map around so the mountains and the distant tower were in the right direction. On the map the road wound around to the right, and far below, in a hollow valley was a vast dark lake.

Harry rolled up the map and he and Marvin were just about to turn to the right when Scarlett shrieked, "Look out!"

They heard a clattering, clanking sound and looked up just in time to see a knight in full armour on horseback, with red and blue livery galloping towards them at full speed. His sword was held high ready for action.

Marvin and Harry leaped to the side as the horseman galloped by. At a bend in the road he turned and galloped back for another pass. This time his visor was up and Harry could see a red, burly face with a huge moustache and side-whiskers.

Harry stepped into the middle of the road and held up his hand. The horse pulled up quickly, throwing the rider forward, then suddenly reared up on its hind legs throwing the rider to the ground with a huge clatter and crash of metal on stone.

Harry and Marvin approached warily while Scarlett flew in to sit in the tree above the fallen warrior. The knight sat still. He'd pulled off his helmet and was rubbing his head. His sword had flown into a bush when he fell, and he scowled at Marvin and Harry.

"Watcha mean scaring my horse like that?" the knight roared.

"And what do you mean charging us like that for no reason?" Harry demanded.

"Defending the territory. My job." The knight retorted.

Harry was furious, "You've no right!". He braced himself for a fight, but he could see that the old man sitting on the ground was no match, so he paused and waited.

The knight heaved himself to his feet and started to march towards Harry.

Marvin stepped between them. "Look, Harry, the man was just doing his job." He turned to the warrior, "Calm down. We're no danger to you. We're just simple travellers."

By this time the knight was face to face with Harry. Neither of them were going to stand down. Then the knight's eyes glanced down to the key on the chain around Harry's neck. He reached for it, and Harry jumped back.

"Get away! The key's mine."

The knight's angry, red face broke into a smile, then a broad grin. Then he started laughing out loud. Suddenly he gave Harry a huge bear hug. The armour dug into Harry's side and back, but he endured the strange behaviour and when the embrace was over said, "What was all that about?"

The knight said, "That key you've got there laddie."

"Yes?"

"I expect you'll be wondering what that strange inscription says."

"Yes. As a matter of fact, I do." Harry was confused.

"Well, I'll bet you my horse that the inscription is written in my native tongue." The knight stretched out his hand, "If you give me the key for a moment, I'll tell you what it says."

Harry's Journal

- As soon as you take action new friends are found.
- Obstacles or opportunities?
- The best way to defeat your enemy is to make him your friend.

Chapter Seven – Facing the Darkness

 Harry pulled back from the knight, "First tell me who you are," he demanded.

"My name is Sir Edmund Breakspeare. I'm sorry I attacked you, but a curse is on me. Because I wrongly killed a man I've been destined to guard this brick pathway against all false travellers, robbers and highwaymen. I automatically attack whoever it is." He hung his head, "I'm afraid I'm not a very successful warrior. I usually fall off my horse just as I did when you stood up to me."

"Why do you want to see the key?" Marvin asked.

"Because the only one who can set me free from my curse is the carrier of the magic key, and I will only know the magic key if the inscription matches the one on my key." At this point he pulled from beneath his armour a key that was identical to Harry's.

Without a word Harry took off his key and handed it to the knight. Sir Edmund examined Harry's key. First he started to laugh quietly, then he fell silent and looked very grim.

"What is it?" Harry asked.

"The inscription is exactly the same as mine," said the knight.

"And what does it say?" Harry asked.

"It says, 'Poverty is the way to treasure, loneliness is the way to love, the way up is down, and darkness is the way to light.'"

"But what does it mean?" Marvin asked.

Scarlett flew down from her tree, "It's a riddle.

"Aye, it is indeed a riddle," said the knight, and I've been here all these years trying to figure it out."

"Harry put his arm around the knight's shoulder, "Why don't you come with us? We're going to the fortress of Baron Blackforze to find the treasure and rescue the princess."

The knight laughed with delight, "I'd love to! You don't know how bored I've been sitting here day in and day out waiting to attack someone for no reason at all."

"You said the bearer the magic key would release you from your curse." Harry said, "How can I do that?"

"Bless you lad! You already have!" said the knight. "I could only be released by a true key bearer inviting me to join his quest, only I couldn't barge in myself. I had to be invited."

"That's settled then," said Marvin, "where do we go next? Scarlett, have you any ideas?"

"Do I have ideas?" Scarlett said, "I have ideas coming out my ears,"

"Parrot," Marvin said, "You don't have any ears."

Scarlett put her beak in the air, "Just a turn of phrase dull one. I suggest you follow the riddle if you want to know where to go next.

"Poverty is the way to the treasure" Harry mused, "Well none of us has much money, so I guess we can tick that box."

"And loneliness is the path to love," said Marvin, "I've never been lonelier than since we set out from home. I've been missing my family and friends."

"True enough" said Sir Edmund, "True enough. Mine's been a lonely task guarding this road all these years."

"The way up is the way down? What's that supposed to mean," said Harry. He pointed to the distant mountains, "That's where we're headed. We need to get up there to the watchtower of Baron Blackforze's fortress. How can we possibly get up there by going down?"

"Aha!" Sir Edmund cried, "Why didn't I think of it before? The road stays on the high ground. It is the easiest way to travel, but if you stay on the high road you will only encounter Blackforze's checkpoints with armed guards. But I've heard that there is a passage through the caves. To get there you must go down through the valley past the Lake of Lethe. The passages go deep through the disused mines, and that will bring us out just beneath the fortress."

"If you knew of this path, why didn't you take it yourself?" Marvin asked the knight.

"You forget. I was cursed to stay here and guard the road. Now I'm free to go with you, and show you the way."

Harry and his friends loaded their packs on Sir Edmund's horse and set off through the forest. As they went deeper into the forest the sky grew dark.

Thunderclouds gathered and before long huge raindrops were splashing around them. The path led downward to a lake at the bottom of a long valley. The lake was still and black. Harry shivered as he thought how deep and dark the water must be. The path wound around the edge of the lake to the entrance to the caves. The rain turned heavy and cold and before long they were trudging along, heads down and drenched through.

Finally they rounded a bend in the lakeside and on a pebbly shore they found the entrance to the caves. It was up a steep incline on the side of a rocky cliff face. As Scarlett and Harry tried to fix a rope to climb up, Marvin and Sir Edmund kept staring across the lake.

Once he got up to the entrance Harry called down, "What's the matter with you two?"

"It's nothing!" Marvin said, as he grabbed the rope and started to climb up. Sir Edmund released the horse, then followed. At the top he kept staring out across the lake, strangely silent. Inside the cave they built a small fire and Marvin cooked bacon and beans for the three of them. Scarlett sat on Harry's shoulder and tucked her head under her wing.

After they had eaten Harry pulled the mirror out of his bag. While Marvin and Sir Edmund were chatting quietly Harry gazed into the mirror. What he saw was terrifying. The vision he'd seen before of a handsome young prince with a golden crown had changed into an unhealthy old king surrounded by gold and jewels, but with a terribly greedy and wicked look in his eyes. As he watched the picture faded and Marvin came into view. This time Marvin was asleep as in the first picture, but he was snoring loudly. He was hugely fat and his bed was surrounded by piles of rotting food. Harry turned the mirror over and quickly put it into his bag.

Harry got up and wandered over to the cave door, but Sir Edmund pulled him back, "I think we'd better not go out there."

"Why not?"

Sir Edmund replied, "As we were coming through the forest I remembered the old stories about the wise ones who live in the lake. The legends say they are beautiful people of light who draw you into the lake with their magic power."

Harry laughed, "Nonsense!" he said, and went to the door. He stared out across the darkened lake. Sir Edmund and Marvin came and stood beside him. As they did a strange blue light began to shine across the surface of the lake and Harry said, "Can you hear the singing? It's beautiful!"

Suddenly there was a terrible squawking and flapping of wings around his head. It was Scarlett, "Don't listen!" She said. "Quick! Come inside! Don't listen!"

Harry, Sir Edmund and Marvin woke out of their trance and hurried back into the cave. At that moment the blue lights materialized into an army of ghostly people—sad, noble creatures clad in ancient robes and wearing crowns that swept up the hill towards the entrance to the caves.

"Quickly!" Sir Edmund called, "Gather your things! Into the caves!"

Scarlett flew ahead while Harry, Marvin and Sir Edmund grabbed their packs. As they hurried into the dark they turned and saw the blue ghosts waiting at the entrance of the cave for their return. Suddenly an icy blast of wind swept through the cave blowing out the fire and chilling them to the heart.

Feeling their way forward in the darkness, they finally escaped the menacing blue lights. They huddled together as Marvin rummaged through his bag for some matches. They made a makeshift torch and looked around them. The passageway they were in led into nine different tunnels— each one leading downward into a dark and confusing labyrinth of the dangerous unknown.

Harry sat down, totally dejected. "We'll never find our way out of here."

"You're right" Marvin said, "There's no way back and there's no way forward."

"You can sit here if you want to," spluttered Sir Edmund, "but, I'm not going to. The riddle said the way to the light was through the darkness. I'm for pushing on. I'm not afraid of the dark. Whatever we discover can't be worse than this!"

At that moment, echoing down the tunnels that lay before them, they heard an unearthly sound—first it sounded like low, insane laughter. Then it grew into a terrible roar before it faded in high pitched wail.

Harry's Journal

- The way up is down.
- Do or Die.
- To discover a new world the old world must die.

Chapter Eight – The Great Ordeal

 "What was that!?" Marvin gasped.

"Why did I ever say that old wizard was boring?" Scarlett squawked, "That life wasn't boring. That was comfortable. I had my food every morning. I could do what I liked. There were no howling monsters waiting to gobble me up. Boring? That wasn't boring…"

The great beast roared again. Louder this time.

Scarlett flew across and perched on Harry's shoulder and tried to hide behind his back, "…OK, it was boring. But who says boring is bad? I like boring. I want boring. Give me boring…"

Harry was terrified. He grabbed Sir Edmund by the arm, "Do you know what's making that terrible sound?"

"It's not your stomach is it?" Sir Edmund said, "Don't tell Marvin I said this, but his cooking's not all that great."

"Seriously, Sir Edmund, What is it?!" Harry pleaded.

The knight paused for a moment, chewed on the edge of his moustache and said, "Sorry. I don't know. No idea."

Harry gazed at the nine different tunnels then turned again to Sir Edmund, "Which way do we go?"

Sir Edmund chewed on his moustache again and said, "Sorry. I don't know. No idea."

Scarlett landed on the knight's head and pecked his bald head, "A fat lot of good you are Sir Breakwind!"

"Don't start fighting!" Marvin said. "If we're going to get through this we'll need to work together. I suggest we try each tunnel one by one, and see where they all go. If they all turn into a dead end, then we try that one..." he pointed to the tunnel from which the beastly howling had come, "the tunnel with Mr. Noisy."

One by one they explored each one of the tunnels. Some ended in a blank wall, some went up into the rock like chimneys, others dropped them down mineshafts into cold pools filled with slime. They worked together, bit by bit to cover every inch of the each tunnel—trying to find the way forward, and all the time avoiding the tunnel where the beast watched and waited. In the darkness they lost track of time. It could have been days or weeks. When they were tired they paused for sleep. When they were hungry they ate.

Eventually they got practised as an efficient team. Scarlett flew ahead with a torch in her beak to scout out the tunnel. Sir Edmund guarded their backs with his sword drawn, while Marvin and Harry took it in turns to try to find a way out. As they went they marked their progress with a piece of chalk, and finally they finished the eighth tunnel. Only one was left: the one where the beast lurked.

"We've been avoiding that monster," said Harry. "We knew deep down that the beast blocked the only way forward. And all we've done is waste time."

"Then there's only one thing for it," said Sir Edmund, "We've got to go forward and face it, whatever it is."

Step by step they went down the last tunnel until at last they crept around a corner and saw it. Two torches burned in wall brackets on either side of a heavy, iron door. In the middle of the door was a large brass keyhole set in an ornate wrought iron setting. In front of the door was a black dog as large as a rhinoceros. He was lying down with his head on his front paws staring at them with large red eyes.

They stopped and stared at the beast. He stared back. Scarlett squeaked, "I don't like the look of those red eyes. They give me the creeps. If this is an adventure I don't want it. I've changed my mind."

"What mind?" Marvin said, "Can't you see the dog is chained up? He can't hurt you."

"Sir Edmund, I have a strange feeling," Harry said, "That one of our keys will probably fit that lock."

Sir Edmund whispered back, "I've had exactly that same feeling. Please…feel free to go first."

"You're too kind." Harry said. "Let's take a moment to think about this."

"I've got an idea!" Scarlett chirped.

"What is it this time?" Marvin moaned.

"Do you see that the chain is fixed to that large pillar over there? Well, if I fly over and get the little puppy's attention he might chase me. I could…Just watch."

With that Scarlett flew off towards the huge beast. The dog jumped up howling and chased Scarlett. She flew towards the pillar, then flew round and round with the great dog chasing her. As it did the chain got shorter and shorter until the dog was trapped with its neck next to the pillar.

"Well done!" Harry called as he and Marvin and Sir Edmund ran to the great door. Sir Edmund's key fit and the door swung open easily. On the other side a stone stairway led up and turned to the left, as they ran up and around they saw the spiral staircase went ever upward further than they could see, but they were spurred on by the fact that at the top there was a glimmer of daylight.

They ran upwards until they ran out of steam, then they kept climbing, pausing for breath, and then they fell to plodding step after endless step, and still the upward climb continued. After another long rest the steps got steeper. They left their bags behind until they were crawling up on all fours.

At last they reached the top of the stairs where a door opened out onto a ledge and a sheer cliff face. Attached to the edge of the ledge was a rickety rope bridge that spanned a gorge that seemed bottomless. On the other side of the bridge was the tower, and at the top window of the tower they just could see a young woman watching their arrival.

Just as they stepped out onto the bridge the door to the tower opened and a knight dressed in jet black armour stepped out, turned and locked the door and threw the key into the canyon. It was Baron Blackforze.

He stared at Harry and his band for what seemed an eternity then said, "You, like many others, have come to get the treasure and rescue the princess. Go home. You will never do it. You will never do it because there is no treasure and there is no princess. There is only this simple tower of mine where I live with my daughter."

Harry stepped onto the rickety bridge and moved forward cautiously. He'd learned not to take things at face value. He approached the villain, and the closer he got, the more vague and shadowy Baron Blackforze became. Then as he approached he saw that he wasn't there at all. Instead there was magic mirror built into the black door, a mirror with an image of a black knight imprinted on it, a mirror that distorted and warped every image as you looked at it. Harry realised that he had been looking at himself, and as soon as the realisation dawned, the Baron had disappeared. He fit the key into the lock and the door sprung open. He ran up the stairs and stopped to gaze at the beautiful girl who was waiting in the tower room.

She smiled down at him, "I was dreaming about you. I knew one day the right people would come together and someone would arrive to rescue me. I've been here ever since the disaster, being looked after by the old butler."

"A butler? But what about Baron Blackforze?"

The girl laughed, "That was just a trick the butler arranged to keep me secure. No one has ever dared to come close enough to the Baron to see that he is really just an illusion."

The girl took Harry by the hand and asked him to sit next to her. "I want to tell you everything, but first I must tell you my name. I am Tessa Sureheart. Who are you? Are you my brother?" At that point she spotted the key around Harry's neck and gasped. She reached for the key, gazed at it and whispered, "You must be my brother. The butler said I had a brother, and that one day he would return with the magic key, and we would be the prince and princess once more."

"A brother?" Harry spluttered, "But…"

His name is Harry. Are you he?

Harry's Journal

- Avoidance magnifies the problem and delays the solution.
- Persistence and Perseverence win the prize.
- Despite your plans, at every stage: Surprises.

Chapter Nine– Claiming the Prize

Tessa gave Harry a huge hug, then gazed at him and stroked his face with her fingers. "It really is you! my long lost brother! We have much to say, but first you and your friends must clean up and rest."

Tessa rang a little silver bell and three handmaids named Faith, Hope and Charity came and let Harry, Marvin and Sir Edmund down a few stairs out into the main part of the palace. They went down a corridor where each was shown a huge room with a hot bath ready and waiting. On the bed, clothes were laid out for them in exactly the right sizes. A short time later Harry met Sir Edmund and Marvin in the corridor. Only then did he realise that Scarlett was missing.

Harry turned to Marvin, "Where's Scarlett?"

At that point a fourth door opened and a beautiful woman with dark skin and jet black hair, stepped into the hall. She was wearing a flowing red floor length dress. Large gold earrings, a solid gold necklace and bangle bracelets gleamed against her rich complexion and completed her amazing appearance. "Is somebody looking for Scarlett?" the woman said.

Harry's jaw dropped wide. "Scarlett??!!"

She smiled broadly, "Did you really think I was just an ordinary bird?" A witch put me under a curse when I was thirteen years old. I laughed at her and kept repeating what she said so she turned me into a parrot. The only way I could shake off the curse was to go on a quest with my true love."

"Your true love??" Harry said.

"If you keep repeating what I say you might get turned into a parrot yourself."

"But how were you supposed to know your true love?" Marvin asked.

"I was told he would come along bearing a large golden key. I must admit," she smiled at Harry, "You didn't seem a very likely prospect when I first saw you."

"You mean it's me?"

"Of course it is", Scarlett smiled. "Now come on, your sister has a fantastic meal waiting."

In the great dining hall Harry heard the whole story of how the kingdom had been taken from his father by three evil lords. Lord Fear, Lord Shame and Lord Anger had kept him enthralled and turned his mind against the people until they rose up and swept him from power installing themselves in his place. The palace butler had escaped with Tessa and kept her safe in the tower, while the palace governess had run with Harry, changed his name and hidden him in the cottage in Over Wandring. After a time the three Lords quarrelled among themselves and the strongest, Lord Fear took over the kingdom. He kept the people enslaved by controlling what they knew and thought of the world.

The dinner went on for a long time. The fine food continued to arrive at the table, the wine flowed, and eventually the candles began to flicker low. Harry couldn't take his eyes off Scarlett. As he gazed at her she caught his eye and smiled back.

Suddenly everything fell into place. He didn't need to marry a princess to become a prince. He was one already, and the whole point of the quest was to discover that fact. He felt a sudden surge in his heart and looked down. The golden key was glowing first a deep golden colour, then it grew hot and turned a reddish gold colour. He knew that Scarlett was to be his princess, and that they would rule his father's kingdom together with Tessa.

At that moment Tessa spoke. "For many long years I have dreamed of your arrival. In my tower room I envisioned the day that we would be reunited. I saw everything, and now the dreams will come to pass." She smiled across at Harry, "I knew that together we would be able to reclaim our father's throne, but I never knew you would bring so many others with you to help. Are your friends willing to help us establish a true and beautiful kingdom once more?"

Harry looked to his friends. Marvin nodded his approval. Sir Edmund gave him a thumbs up. "I know these friends are with us," Harry said, "but our team is incomplete without the others. We need Sarge and Gloria Goodbody."

"What about Farmer Doubtfire? Marvin asked. "We could use a man with common sense."

"Don't forget Father Dominus" Scarlett said. We need

his wisdom, his magic and his learning."

"But who are these people and how can we get them here?" Tessa asked.

Harry said, "Marvin, do you remember Father Dominus spoke to us through that little mirror? Maybe he'll do it again."

"Yes!" Marvin said, and ran off to get the mirror. In a moment he was in the hall. He placed the mirror on the table in front of them. As the candlelight flickered, the mirror darkened, then the face of Dominus Maginot appeared and they heard his voice, "Well done Harry! Victory at last. Now what will you do?"

Harry put his arm around Scarlett's waist. "I'm going to enjoy the fruits of my labours!" Suddenly Maginot disappeared from the mirror and Harry saw once more the image of himself as a fat, greedy old king. Maginot's voice thundered from the rafters, "Victory is not for the victor."

"But isn't that what being a hero is all about?" Harry asked.

"The word 'hero'" Maginot said, "Means, 'one who makes a sacrifice.'"

One by one the candles guttered out and the friends drifted into silence. Maginot's face flickered up in the mirror again. He too was silent and grave.

Finally Harry said in a very faint voice, "What does the hero sacrifice?"

In a quiet voice Maginot said, "Himself."

Harry was silent.

"You have gone on this journey not to create another Ordinary World of your own comfort and ease, but to continue from this adventure to another."

Tessa stood up and lit the candles, "You see, the whole kingdom, including the village of Over Wandring is in the thrall of Lord Fear." She looked around, "Can we set out together to rid the land of this tyrant?"

Harry stood up, "I will go. Who will go with me?"

Harry's Journal

- Victory is not for the Victor.
- A hero is 'one who makes a sacrifice.'

Chapter Ten – A New Level of Life

 As soon as he said it, Harry felt another surge of energy and strength. Marvin stood up and raised his glass in the air, "I'm with you."

"And me too," said Sir Edmund.

Scarlett stood by Harry's side and took his arm, "You're certainly not setting out on another adventure without me."

Tessa stood at the head of the table, She was beautiful in her long black dress with purple trim. "I will go with you brother, and if I cannot be your queen, for I see that place is taken, I will be your princess royal."

At that moment there was a huge crash, a blaze of light and a puff of green smoke. When the smoke had cleared Dominus Maginot was standing in the room with one arm around a very bewildered looking Farmer Doubtfire and his other arm around a stern, but satisfied looking Sarge.

Harry ran up to greet them all when he was knocked down by another minor explosion. The window blew open, a ball of blue light flew into the centre of the room, spun around three times and lit on the table. As they stared the blue ball of light faded and Gloria Good body stepped forth brushing down her dress, "I've got some time free, dearies. Thought I could use a break from all this good fairy business and come with you on the quest." She looked at Harry, "This one's going to make your first outing look like a walk in the park. I reckon that was just practice for the real thing. You'll need someone to help out here and there—someone to talk to, a shoulder to cry on—well, old Gloria Goodbody's here to help."

Tessa clapped her hands. More candles were brought. The fire was stoked up. The newcomers sat at the table and the feast continued.

Harry sat at the head of the table with Tessa, "If we are going to succeed we need to have a plan" Harry said. "Father Maginot, what shall we do?"

"Each of you has different strengths," the old magician said. "So each of you will contribute to the team best, not by being someone else, but by being all that you can be. There are nine of you. Together you complete one another. Like instruments in an orchestra, all of you must together produce music that is greater than the sum of all it parts."

"Now what's that supposed to mean?" Farmer Doubtfire muttered to Marvin.

"What it means Tom Doubtfire," the magician said, "is that alone we are incomplete. Together we become more than we can be on our own. We need each other if the adventure is to continue. There are nine of us, and this mystical number of three repeated three times will lead all of us to wholeness if we take time to understand."

"But we have a job to do. We don't have time for study," said Scarlett.

"Precisely. The sort of wisdom I am speaking of is the

understanding that comes from action, not from study. We learn by doing, even if that means we learn by painful error."

The conversation went on far into the night as the fellowship made their plans to take back the kingdom.

One by one the nine characters left the room until Harry was left alone with the old magician. They sat in silence staring at the fire until Dominus Maginot got up, crossed the room, opened the big double doors and went out onto the balcony.

Harry followed him and stood looking out across the valley. A large silver moon and tiny stars glowed in the night sky.

"What have you learned most from your adventure Harry?"

Harry thought for a moment. "I'm not really sure. I suppose that I was a prince all along, but I had to go on the journey to discover the fact."

"True enough." Said the old wizard, "Is there anything else?"

Harry thought for a moment and said, "I've learned that there is no substitute for the journey. Thinking about it, dreaming about it and planning it are not the same thing as doing it."

"True enough," the magician muttered, "True enough, and was the journey as you had planned?"

Harry laughed, "Far from it! There was far more to it than I could have imagined. The adventure itself was as different as a map is from the journey itself."

Harry paused and thought for a moment, then said, "I suppose the other thing is that I have discovered the true meaning of the quest."

"And what is that?"

"The journey was not about the princess or the kingdom, or the treasure or the red coach with silver wheels or the fine palace."

"If the journey was not about that, what was it about?"

Harry looked up at the magician with a radiant smile and said, "It was about becoming an Ordinary Hero."

The Ordinary Hero Workbook

The *Hero's Map of Achievement* is the ten stage map of the change process. Harry followed the ten stages as each chapter of the story unfolded. This simple map provides an outline for any kind of change you wish to make. You can apply the map to small scale personal change, change within your family or community, or change within your company or your world.

Of course real, permanent change is far more complex than this simple ten stage map – just as a real journey is far more complicated and unpredictable than the map you use for the journey. Nevertheless, maps are important tools for the journey, and The *Hero's Map of Achievement* is a map that is deeply rooted in the understanding of the whole human race.

The Ordinary Hero Workbook explains the ten stages of the *Hero's Map of Achievement* in more detail, and gives a set of questions and quotations to help you apply the principles to your own situation.

Next time you read *The Magic Key* keep a marker in the workbook and see how Harry's story takes him through the *Hero's Map of Achievement* step by step. Then use the questions and quotations to empower your own quest to become an Ordinary Hero.

Stage One – The Ordinary World

The Ordinary World is where we start the journey. We're surrounded with a contented clan of family, friends and colleagues. The Ordinary World is our comfort zone, but within that world we're restless. We sense there is more to life. We want more, but we're not sure what we really want, and we don't know where to start. The idea of an adventure seems too much trouble; so we carry on our regular day to day existence. Then something bursts into our life to kick-start the adventure.

Questions:
1. What is your Ordinary World?
2. Who is your contented clan?
   a. What's good about the contented clan?
   b. What's bad about the contented clan?
3. What are your dreams for the future?
4. What has happened, or might happen to kick-start your adventure?

Most men pass their lives in a state of quiet desperation
–Thoreau

Most of us are living in the basement of a thousand room palace – *Harry Moody*

Stage Two – Hearing the Call

The comfort zone has been invaded! At this stage we ask what we really want. This makes us ask what we believe. Do we believe in fate which means we can do nothing about our future, or do we believe in destiny— which means we can take charge of change? The Ordinary Hero starts to realise that there is only one person who will make change happen: <u>himself</u>. We begin by paying attention to our dreams, and turning our unrealistic dreams into a clear vision. Next we turn the vision into goals, and the goals into 'now actions'— something we can do today that doesn't rely on anyone else.

Questions:

1. What do you really want? What would you do if you were not afraid?
2. Do you believe in fate or destiny?
3. Who is responsible for making positive change happen?
4. How can you change your dreams into a realistic vision?
5. 'Now Actions' are positive steps that rely on nobody else for their success. What actions can you take today?

Beliefs are what cause some individuals to become heroes, while others 'lead lives of quiet desperation'
– *Anthony Robbins*

What lies behind us and what lies before us are tiny matters compared to what lies within us.
– *William Morrow*

Stage Three – Refusing the Call

 *At first the call seems exciting, then we realise what the adventure will cost and say, "I can't do that, I won't do that." Sometimes we act out this refusal by making an enthusiastic start, only to reach an obstacle, turn around and head home. Most of us stop at this point, give up and settle for the ordinary world. The Ordinary Hero, on the other hand, works through this stage. Although it feels bad, the refusal of the call is where important questions are raised. The questions reveal the problems we need to overcome before we can start the journey. There are three sorts of problems: barriers, people problems and our inner doubts and fears.*

Questions:

1. What kind of false starts have you made on the journey?
2. Why did you give up? What went wrong?
3. Barriers are real problems. What barriers stand in your way?
4. What people problems do you face? Who is holding you back?
5. What are your inner doubts and fears?

The unexamined life is not worth living – *Plato*

Follow your bliss – *Joseph Campbell*

Stage Four – Meeting the Mentor

 *The 'mentor' is any person or resource that helps us answer the questions that came up in stage three. The mentor gives information, training and encouragement, and challenges us to leave the comfort zone and become all that we can be.*

In the great stories, the mentor is a wise old man or woman because their gifts are experience and insight. The mentor is a magical figure because the gifts he provides seem strange and powerful to the hero.

Questions:

1. The questions you asked at the last stage help you decide what sort of mentor you need.
2. What challenges will your mentor present?
3. What gifts will your mentor have for you? How might the mentor help you overcome your barriers, your people problems and your doubts and fears?
4. What other training, equipment, or information do you need?

The first encounter of the hero journey is with a protective figure (often a little old crone or an old man) who provides the adventurer with special gifts. – *Joseph Campbell*

How can you expect to get the right answers if you are not asking the right questions? – *Ben Stauffer*

Stage Five – Crossing the Threshold

We've set the goals, we've confronted our doubts, and the mentor has given us gifts for the journey. At last we're ready to take the plunge. At this stage we check our target, weigh the risks, and then take the step across the threshold into the world of adventure.

Almost at once the hero stumbles and falls, but it doesn't matter how often we fall, but how often we get up.

Questions:
1. What is the commitment you're making?
2. Are you ready for a step into the unknown?
3. What must you do to minimise the risk?
4. You may fall as soon as you step out. Are you prepared for a crash landing?

It is in your moments of decision that your destiny is shaped. – *Anthony Robbins*

If you don't risk anything you risk even more.
– *Erica Jong*

Walking is Controlled Falling.

Stage Six – Trials, Allies and Enemies

Immediately after we step into the world of adventure we meet new friends. These are people who are also on the adventure. However, these new friends are unlike anyone we've ever thought of as friends before. We also meet our first problems, and through these challenges we learn more about ourselves and other people. This helps us to become leaders, and discover how to build a team around us. We also face our first enemies, how to recognise them and how to deal with them.

Questions:

1. Where will you find the team of people who are already on the journey?
2. How are they like you? How are they different from you?
3. How can their differences complete rather than clash with you?
4. Do you see difficulties as obstacles or opportunities?
5. Who are your real allies? Who are the real enemies?

The hero goes on his quest alone, then suddenly finds that he is part of an army on the move. – *Ben Stauffer*

There is no security on this earth, only opportunity.
– *Douglas McArthur*

Stage Seven – Facing the Darkness

After the initial success we face the real sacrifice required for long lasting success. At this point we want more than anything to turn back to the comfort of our Ordinary World, but we realise that we've already burnt our bridges. There are only two options: fall over the edge into ruin or climb over the edge to safety and success. The threats, difficulties and challenges also bring us face to face with our inner faults and difficulties.

Questions:

1. How do you respond when the way becomes dark and confusing?
2. What is the real price of success?
3. What sort of darkness will you face on the journey?
4. What sort of inner demons have you kept locked away?
5. Where will you find help to face the inner demons?

I am not afraid of storms for I am learning how to sail my ship – *Louise May Allcott*

The hero grows from his wound – *Bart Gavigan*

Stage Eight – The Great Ordeal

The eighth stage of the journey is the long, hard, slog. At this stage we have to acquire perseverance and persistence. We have to work harder than we ever imagined it was possible to work. We have to learn to be realistic about our goals, our friends and ourselves. We have to build a hard working and dedicated team around us. Through this stage we make slow progress, but each step takes us closer to the goal.

Questions:

1. How do you deal with details?
2. How do you deal with disappointment?
3. Can you really work hard and persevere to the end?
4. For the hero, battle is inevitable. How do you deal with conflict?
5. Are you realistic about others, about yourself, about the journey?

We do not have to become heroes overnight. Just a step at a time, meeting each thing that comes up, seeing it is not as dreadful as it appeared, discovering we have the strength to stare it down. – *Eleanor Roosevelt*

Life without war is impossible… The basis of physical, mental, moral, and spiritual growth is antagonism… This is the open fact of life. – *Oswald Chambers*

Stage Nine – Claiming the Prize

What a great feeling! We've reached the goal and claim the prize. The task was harder than we imagined and the adventure more exciting and costly than we ever would have guessed. That makes the taste of victory even sweeter. But there's an aftertaste. We have the prize, but there's still an empty feeling. We're still looking for something. We still have questions. What was the prize for? What are we supposed to do with the prize now we've got it? What next?

Questions

1. After getting what we want, why do we still feel restless?
2. What else did you get besides the prize you set out for?
3. Is the prize worth it? Can you cope with success?
4. Who is the prize for?

It's easier to get what you think you want than to know what you really want – *Ben Stauffer*

What does it profit a man if he gains the whole world, but loses his soul? – *Jesus Christ*

Satge Ten – A New Level of Life

At the end of the journey we realise the journey was not about a pot of gold or the dream marriage or the perfect career. It was about becoming an Ordinary Hero. An Ordinary Hero is a fulfilled person—a person who is able to live ordinary life in a heroic way. The adventure was in the outer world, but at heart it was an inner journey of personal transformation. The Ordinary Hero has a new attitude to life. Every day is a new adventure. Every moment is an opportunity for growth and learning. The Ordinary Hero realises that the end of one journey is the beginning of another. Have you reached the end of the journey? Brace yourself! There's more to come!

Questions:
1. What have you learned from the journey?
2. What was the journey for?
3. Is this the end, or a new beginning?
4. Where do I go from here?

Do not wish to be anything but what you are, and to be that perfectly – *St Francis de Sales*

Life is painting a picture, not doing a sum.
– *Oliver Wendall Holmes*

The journey is the reward. – *Lao Tzu*

Hero's map of achievement...

Harry's Roller Coaster Ride

The Hero's Map of Achievement is illustrated by the ministory of Harry's Roller Coaster Ride. Using the picture opposite, see how Harry moves from the Ordinary World of relaxing with a cool drink in the theme park to face the adventure of the roller coaster. He refuses the call with all sorts of excuses, then meets a friend who encourages him to go on the roller coaster. Each stage of the journey follows on from there, to illustrate all ten steps of the Hero's Map of Achievement.

Full colour copies of Harry's Roller Coaster Ride are available free of charge. Simply be in touch by email through the Ordinary Hero Website: www.ordinaryhero.net.

This illustration of the Hero's Map of Achievement is also available in poster size, laminated placemats, mousemats and mugs. All of them are excellent ways to remind you and your team of the ten stages of the *Hero's Map of Achievement*. You can order them through the Ordinary Hero website.

How to Be an Ordinary Hero

Dwight Longenecker and his team run a range of courses helping people learn how to be Ordinary Heroes. Illustrated with clips from Hollywood films, the Ordinary Hero programme is accessible and exciting for all ages and levels of education. Through the use of films it engages participants with visual impact, packs an emotional punch and applies the lessons through creative learning activities.

Ordinary Hero at Work is a company that uses the Ordinary Hero programme to transform businesses. The programme builds dynamic teams, motivates workers and empowers the lasting change that brings higher efficiency and a workforce with direction and drive, resulting in decreased staff turnover and higher profits.

The Ordinary Hero programme is also used as a personal growth method. Through regular courses and personal coaching, individuals use the vocabulary and method of Ordinary Hero to change their world for the better.

The Ordinary Hero charity uses the same programme to help people on the margins of society. Through Ordinary Hero prisoners prepare for a new life once their sentence ends. It is also used for young people with drugs problems, victims of violent crime and people on 'back to work' programmes.

Members of the public can experience the power of the Ordinary Hero's Quest through a special three day seminar that illustrates the ten stages of the Hero's Map of Achievement with special film clips. The three day Quest also takes you on the adventure of learning more about your personality type through the profiling system, Ordinary Hero Character Roles.

If you would like to know more about Ordinary Hero at Work, or any of the other Ordinary Hero programmes, log on to our website: www.ordinaryhero.net.

Order more copies of
How to Be an Ordinary Hero

How to Be an Ordinary Hero is a perfect gift for individuals or whole groups of people. The book is easy enough for everyone to read while the ideas are life changing for all. Whole organisations can be transformed once everyone shares a new way of seeing the challenge of change. Share this new vocabulary for change by buying copies for teams at work, family members and members of your committees, charities and church groups.

You can order more copies of *How to Be an Ordinary Hero* through our website. The retail selling price of *How to Be an Ordinary Hero* is £5.00 or $10.00. There are significant discounts for bulk orders of 50 or more.

Nine Ways to Be an Ordinary Hero

Do you remember the nine main characters from *The Magic Key?*

- ■ Marion Doright
- ■ Gloria Goodbody
- ■ Harry Dashwood
- ■ Tessa Sureheart
- ■ Dominus Maginot
- ■ Farmer Doubtfire
- ■ Scarlett the Parrot
- ■ Sir Edmund Breakspeare
- ■ Marvin Makepeace

Each character represents one of the nine personality types in the special profiling system called *Ordinary Hero Character Roles.*

Watch out for Dwight Longenecker's next book called *Nine Ways to Be an Ordinary Hero.* You'll meet all nine characters again and they'll help you understand the nine personality types. A special quiz will reveal which personality type is most like you.

Understanding your personality type helps you understand and master your deepest motivations in life. *Nine*

Ways to Be an Ordinary Hero will also help you understand your work colleagues, family members and friends.
It will show you how to use the powerful impulses that
drive your life to empower your own hero's quest and lead
you to a fuller and richer life.

For special preview copies of *Nine Ways to Be an
Ordinary Hero* make contact through the Ordinary Hero
website: www.ordinaryhero.net.

Dwight Longenecker

The founder of Ordinary Hero, Dwight Longenecker is an American based in England. He is a freelance writer with eight books to his credit. He contributes to a range of magazines and papers on both sides of the Atlantic.

Dwight is also the author of four business training video packages, and multi media scripts for the British Council.

With a degree in Speech and English he is a skilled and enthusiastic presenter. Through his training at the National Film and Television School, and in scriptwriting master classes, Dwight became familiar with the hero's quest, and refined the hero's journey into the ten stage *Hero's Map of Achievement©*.

Research and training in the Enneagram with Don Riso and Russ Hudson helped him develop *Ordinary Hero Character Roles*. In seminars and coaching he applies these tools for business growth and personal development.

To learn more contact www.ordinaryhero.net